FEATHERS Not Just for Flying

Melissa Stewart • Illustrated by Sarah S. Brannen

ını Charlesbridge

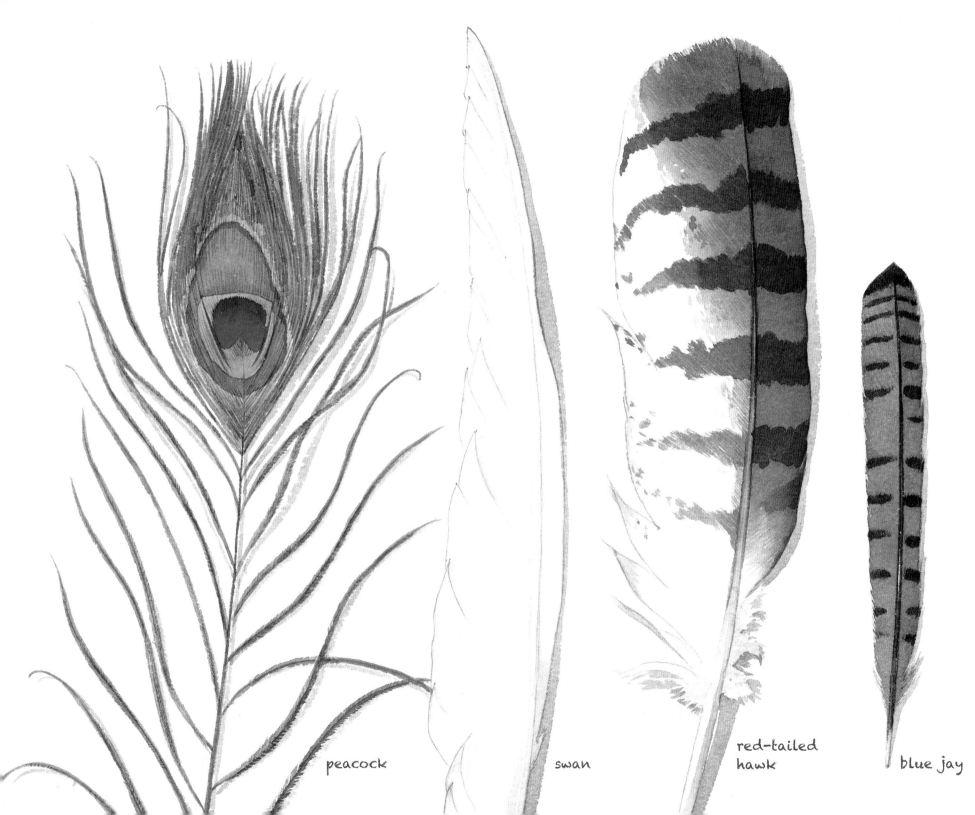

peacock

swan

red-tailed
hawk

blue jay

Birds and feathers go together, like trees and leaves, like stars and the sky. All birds have feathers, but no other animals do.

Most birds have thousands of feathers, but those feathers aren't all the same. That's because feathers have so many different jobs to do.

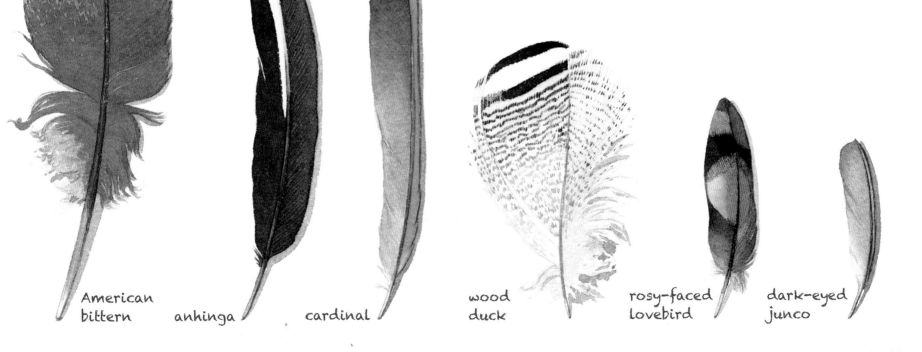

American bittern

anhinga

cardinal

wood duck

rosy-faced lovebird

dark-eyed junco

Feathers can warm like a blanket . . .

On cold, damp days a blue jay stays warm by fluffing up its feathers and trapping a layer of warm air next to its skin.

Blue jay, Bradbury Mountain, Maine

Wood duck, Lake Bemidji, Minnesota

or cushion like a pillow.

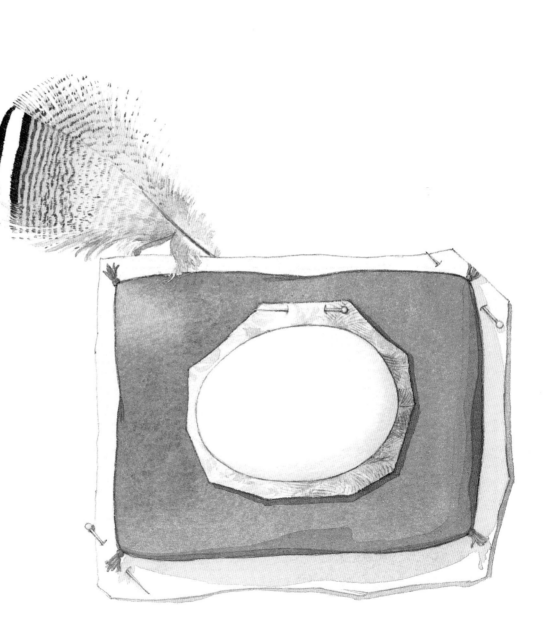

A female wood duck lines her nest with feathers she plucks from her own body. These feathers cushion the duck's eggs and keep them warm.

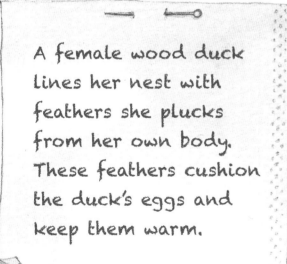

Feathers can shade out sun like an umbrella . . .

As a hungry tricolored heron wades through the water in search of food, it raises its wings high over its head. The feathers block out reflections from the sky and shade the water. This makes it easier to spot tasty fish and frogs.

Tricolored heron, Florida Everglades

Red-tailed hawk, Shiprock, New Mexico

or protect skin like sunscreen.

On sunny summer afternoons red-tailed hawks spend hours soaring through the sky in search of prey. Their thick feathers protect their delicate skin from the sun's harmful rays.

SUNBLOCK
SPF 30
sun protection

Feathers can soak up water like a sponge . . .

On sizzling summer days a male sandgrouse cools off by soaking his belly feathers in a watering hole. Then the proud papa flies to his nest. While dad guards his chicks, the little ones suck on his feathers to quench their thirst.

Pallas's sandgrouse, Gobi Desert, Mongolia

or clean up messes like a scrub brush.

An American bittern always cleans up after it eats. Its feathers have brittle tips that crumble into a dusty powder. The powder is perfect for scouring away the dirt and slimy fish oil that sticks to its feathers.

American bittern,
Tualatin River, Oregon

1.3

SCRUBBY

Feathers can distract attackers like a bullfighter's cape…

A dark-eyed junco distracts its enemies by flashing the bright white feathers on the outside of its tail. Then it quickly covers the feathers and darts off in the other direction.

Dark-eyed junco, Lincoln, Massachusetts

or hide a bird from predators like camouflage clothing.

A female cardinal's dull, grayish-tan body and feathers blend in with her forest home. They help her hide and protect her nest from enemies while she sits on her eggs.

Northern cardinal, Columbus, Ohio

Feathers can make high-pitched sounds like a whistle ...

When a male club-winged manakin wants to get a female's attention, he leans forward, raises his wings over his back, and rapidly shakes them. As feathers with ridges rub against feathers with stiff, curved tips, a squeaky chirping sound trills through the air.

Club-winged manakin, Milpe Bird Sanctuary, Ecuador, South America

Peacock, Pusa Hill Forest, New Delhi, India

or attract attention like fancy jewelry.

A peacock's bright, beautiful tail feathers make him easy to spot. At mating time a female is attracted to the male with the biggest, most colorful fan of feathers.

Feathers can dig holes like a backhoe . . .

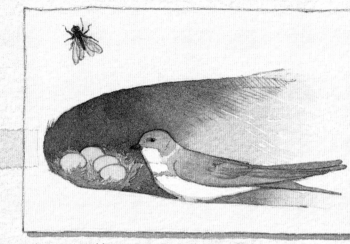

After bank swallows mate they make a home together. First the male uses his bill and the tough feathers on his lower legs to dig a two-foot-long tunnel in a stream bank. He pushes the dirt out with his wings. Then the female builds a nest of straw, grasses, and leaves at the end of the tunnel.

Bank swallow, Bear River, Utah

or carry building supplies like a forklift.

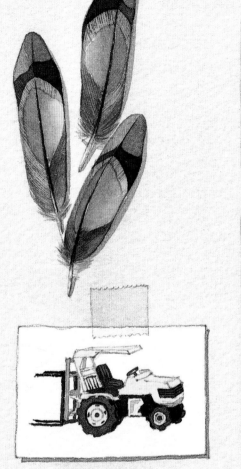

Rosy-faced lovebird, Guab River, Namibia, Africa

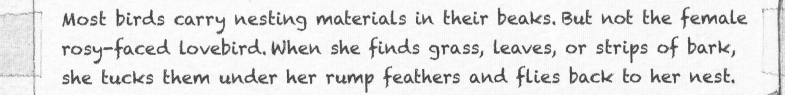

Most birds carry nesting materials in their beaks. But not the female rosy-faced lovebird. When she finds grass, leaves, or strips of bark, she tucks them under her rump feathers and flies back to her nest.

Feathers can help birds float like a life jacket . . .

Mute swans glide smoothly across the water's surface. Pockets of air trapped between their feathers help these graceful birds stay afloat.

Mute swan, Chesapeake Bay, Maryland

Anhinga, Lake Martin, Louisiana

or plunge downward like a fishing sinker.

Most birds make a special oil to waterproof their feathers, but not the anhinga. The weight of its wet feathers helps the hungry hunter dive deep down in search of fish, crayfish, and shrimp.

Feathers can glide like a sled . . .

Emperor penguins have tightly packed belly feathers that form firm, slick surfaces. The feathers make it easy for these birds to slide across ice and snow.

Emperor penguin, Adélie Land, Antarctica

or sprint across the snow like snowshoes.

Each autumn, willow ptarmigans grow a thick layer of feathers on top of their toes. Like snowshoes the feathers increase the size of the birds' feet, so they can shuffle across the snow instead of sinking in.

Willow ptarmigan, Denali National Park, Alaska

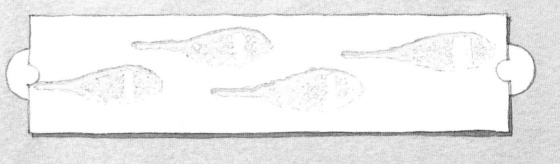

But most of all, feathers can give birds
the lift they need to race across the sky.

Kinds of Feathers

Many scientists study birds, and they are learning new information every day. Right now not all scientists agree about the best way to classify types of feathers. Here is one system that many scientists use:

Tiny filoplume feathers are attached to nerves. They help a bird sense its surroundings, and they let the bird know that its feathers are in place.

Stiff bristle feathers around a bird's eyes act like eyelashes. Some birds use bristle feathers around their mouths to locate food.

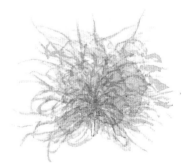

Soft, fluffy down feathers keep a bird warm by trapping body heat next to its skin.

Semiplume feathers work with down feathers to keep birds warm and dry.

Contour feathers cover most of a bird's body. They give a bird its shape and colors.

The flight feathers on a bird's wings lift it up and move it forward. Flight feathers on the tail help a bird steer and keep its balance.

Author's Note

While I was doing research for another book, I stumbled across a fascinating article in *Birder's World* (now *BirdWatching* magazine). It described some of the amazing ways birds use their feathers. I knew this would be a great topic for a children's book, so I photocopied the article and pinned it to the idea board in my office.

A few months later I dug into the research. As I do for all my books, I turned to three main sources for information: the library (for books, magazines, and newspapers), the Internet (for journal articles and locating experts in the field), and my own nature journals. Some examples in this book are based on my personal observations in the natural world. Others come from interviews with scientists as well as reports in scholarly books and scientific journals.

For me, research is the easy part of a project. The hard part is figuring out the most interesting way to frame the material. I'm always asking myself, "Is there a way I can make this even more engaging?" For this book, I spent three years tinkering with the text. I wrote countless drafts and did four complete overhauls before I finally latched on to the idea of comparing feathers to common objects in our lives. That's when the writing came to life, and I knew the manuscript was ready for my editor.

Text copyright © 2014 by Melissa Stewart
Illustrations copyright © 2014 by Sarah S. Brannen
All rights reserved, including the right of reproduction in whole or in part in any form.
Charlesbridge and colophon are registered trademarks of Charlesbridge Publishing, Inc.

Published by Charlesbridge
85 Main Street
Watertown, MA 02472
(617) 926-0329
www.charlesbridge.com

Library of Congress Cataloging-in-Publication Data
Stewart, Melissa.
    Feathers : not just for flying/Melissa Stewart; illustrated by Sarah S. Brannen.
        p. cm.
    Includes bibliographical references and index.
    ISBN 978-1-58089-430-2 (reinforced for library use)
    ISBN 978-1-58089-431-9 (softcover)
    ISBN 978-1-60734-627-2 (ebook pdf)
1. Feathers—Juvenile literature. 2. Birds—Behavior—Juvenile literature.
I. Brannen, Sarah S., illustrator. II. Title.

QL697.4.S74 2013
598.147—dc23   2012038694

Printed in Singapore
(hc) 10 9 8 7 6 5 4 3 2
(sc) 10 9 8 7 6 5 4 3 2 1

Illustrations done in watercolor on Saunders Waterford cold-press paper
Display type set in Textile by Apple Computer, Inc.
Text type set in Frogster by Typotheticals
Color separations by KHL Chroma Graphics, Singapore
Printed by Imago in Singapore
Production supervision by Brian G. Walker
Designed by Diane M. Earley